Jesus Is Looking Down

"On A Sinful World"

Jesus Is Looking Down

"On A Sinful World"

By:

Evangelist Dr. Florine Walker

ARPress
ILLUMINATING IDEAS,
EMPOWERING VOICES.

ARPress LLC
45 Dan Road Suite 5
Canton MA 02021
Hotline: 1(888) 821-0229
Fax: 1(508) 545-7580

Ordering Information:
Quantity sales. Special discounts are available on quantity purchases by corporations, associations, and others. For details, contact the publisher at the address above.

Printed in the United States of America.

ISBN-13:	Softcover	979-8-89356-534-8
	eBook	979-8-89356-535-5

Library of Congress Control Number: 2024902548

Contents

Dedication

I want to thank my husband, Eugene,
who always encouraged me, and tells me to
go for it; he is one of my biggest supporters.

I have wonderful children, so I dedicate this
Book to my five sons and two daughters,
Emmett/Betty, Mike, Ron, Quentin/Sandra,
Jeff, Cynthia and Jacqueline.

I thank my brothers, sisters
And extended family.

Lastly but not the least, to my grandchildren;

and in memories of my parents
Mary Fabian and Willie Andrews.

Graditude

Bishop Jerry McCullough

Sis Maggie

Dr. Jordan

Prophetess Debra

Reverend James McGriff

Sis Joyce

Reverend James Watkins

Sis Mag

Introduction

I feel deep within my heart that I was obligated to write about the vision that I had of Jesus.

I want people to know that God is alive, and that He still reveals and talks to his people in this age.

God is a God of love, compassion; and there are times when the good suffers with the bad; and no matter what happens, good will always come out of bad.

We will never understand and know why God allows good people to die in horrible situation. I am sure He will answer all of our questions when we get to heaven. We serve a God who is too wise to make a mistake.

The words of the preacher, teacher, the son of King David states, the thing that hath been, it is that which shall be done; and there is no new thing under the sun (Ecc.1:9).

One thing I notice after the shooting at Columbine, was that different catastrophes occurred in succession, one right after another and not only in America, but in other parts of the words. We are still seeing all kinds of frightening and devastating events as I write this book.

Amos 3:7 states, surely the Lord will do nothing, but he revealeth his secret unto his servants the prophets.

A Vision At 5:00 AM

God began showing me visions as a little girl, and showing me different things in dreams, not regularly but on occasion.

And it shall come to past in the last days, saith God, I will pour out my spirit upon all flesh; and your sons and your daughter shall prophesy, and your young men shall see visions and your old men shall dream dreams (Acts 2:17).

And on my servants and on my hand-maidens I will pour out in those days of my spirit, and they shall prophesy (Acts 2:18);

And I will show wonders in heaven above, and signs in the earth beneath; blood, and fire, and vapors of smoke (Acts 2:19).

Many people will never completely understand visions and dreams, I must say, that God is the same God today that He was in the days of Abraham, Isaac, and Jacob.

In 1998, I was in the bed, not asleep but just lying there; it was 5:00 am. In the spirit I see myself standing at my back door, looking up toward the sky; and there stood above the clouds, the Christ with a rod in one hand and a sickle in the other hand. The cloud was above His Knees, His upper body was visible, and He seems to be leaning forward looking over us the U.S (or the world). He had displeased look on his face. There is no doubt in my mind this was my lord; my savior Jesus Christ. I must say that Jesus is very much alive; I must say this over and over again. He appears to some, in dreams or in visions, in this present age.

What is a vision? A vision is something seen otherwise than by ordinary sight (as in a dream or a trance) unusual wisdom in foreseeing what is going to happen.

One must understand that God is a God of love, but He is also a God of wrath. Wickedness and sin brings about death and destruction.

God always warns his people beforehand. He used men and women of God to sound the alarm. We have many people who just don't get it. They will not get it until trouble is upon them.

God's Judgement Upon The Land

In the days of Noah, God saw that the wickedness of man was great in the earth and that every imagination of the thoughts of his heart was only evil continually.

And it repented the Lord that he had made man on the earth, and it grieved him in his heart.

And God said I will destroy man, whom I have created from the face of the earth; not only man, but beast, and creeping things, and the fowl of the air (Gen. 6:5-7).

Noah founded grace in the eyes of God, for he was a righteous man. Moreover, because Noah was a righteous man and obeyed the Lord, Noah and his family life was spared from the flood.

God's Covenant – The Rainbow

God made an everlasting covenant with Noah and every living creature that was with him. He said the water shall no more become a flood to destroy all flesh (Gen. 9:15). God did not say, there would be no more floods. He is saying that he will not use a flood to destroy all of mankind again.

> God said unto Noah this is the covenant I have established between me and all flesh that is upon the earth (Gen. 9:17).

There are times, when you look up into the sky after a rainstorm, you will notice a beautiful bow, God, who is loving, full of mercy, and who will hear us when we cry unto him; repent and change our ways.

God Is The Only True God

In America everyone is allowed to worship and serve their (God) god, and it is one of the best places in the world to live. But America has allowed too many sacrifices to be made. We stood by and prayer was taken out of our schools, we have allowed the Ten Commandments to be removed from the public sight, we are not allowed to display any Christian arts, pictures or even a cross on buildings. What is going on in this country? We who are believers of the true and living God need to speak up, men; women in authority, and government officials need to speak out against the evilness that is taking place in this great country.

People who feel offended by prayer and religious display, should move to another country. If you live in any other, you will obey the rules- laws of that country. For instance, if you lived in (the Middle East,) Iran, you would not say to the leader, remove your Muslim symbols or I will sue you. You would not say to the Emperor of China, remove Buddha from display, because I promise, there would be a punishment.

Wake Up America

In the New Testament, the scripture speaks about the Lord and His destruction upon the unrighteous. Many today are denying the word of God.

> (2 Peter 2:2-3) And many shall follow their pernicious ways; by reason of whom the way of truth shall be evil spoken of.
>
> And through covetousness shall they feigned words make merchandise of you: whose judgement now of along time lingereth not, and their damnation slumbereth not.

America we must be very careful of those who are working to destroy our country, the enemy is using all of his tricks, that being tricks in his bag in order to destroy this great nation.

One of his first tricks was to remove discipline and prayer out of school and we can see the terrible effect that had on our children. The second trick was to introduce drugs to the younger generations, and the attitude that anything goes. This did not happen overnight.

Americans must pray. For this great nation, for our president and all government officials. I believe that it is time for Christians all over this country and the world to repent, and declare a day of fasting that includes prayer. Even the leaders shouldn't be exempted. We are sitting around allowing sin to run rampant in this country. It is praying time. We must pray that America return to what this country was founded on, which are good moral principles, not the evil that transpired, but to Godly principles. God hates sin. Adam and Eve our first biological parents sinned. They set sin in motion, because of their disobedience.

> God commanded Adam saying, of every tree of the garden thou mayest freely eat; but tree of knowledge of good and evil thou shall not eat of it; for the day that thou eatest, therefore thou shalt surely die (Gen. 2:16).

When Adam disobeyed God that action brought change into the life of Adam and Eve and mankind.

When Man Turns Away From God

A perfect example of wickedness is what transpired in Sodom and Gamorrah, God destroyed both cities.

> But the men of Sodom were wicked and sinners before the Lord exceedingly (Gen. 13:13); God rained upon the cities fire and brimstone (Gen. 19:24, 25).

We do not understand everything that God does, or why he allows it to happen. But one thing I do know is that sin is an offense against God. God, who is a God of compassion, sometimes gets angry. In the vision previously mentioned, He had a displeased look on his face, a look that I will never forget. I truly believe that God is trying to get our attention; He is giving us a chance to change the direction we are going. The mass murderers, earthquakes, storms, fires and mudslides etc. are God's way of getting our attention.

I do not pretend to have all of the answers, and I am not saying that God is so very angry that He is going to destroy everybody at this time. No one knows when the end shall come, except God.

> In the Gospel (of Luke 21: 8-11), Christ states, take heed that you be not deceived; for many shall come in my name, saying I am the Christ; and the time draw near, go ye not after them.
>
> But when you shall hear of wars and commotions, be not terrified; for these things must first come to pass, but the end is not [at once].
>
> And great earthquakes shall be in different places, and famines, and pestilences; and fearful sights and great signs shall there be from heaven.

We are living in the days of all the above, but we who are children of God need not fear, we ought to watch and pray, and continue in the work of the Lord. We must compel those, who are not saved to accept Christ as their savior.

Jonah Had A Word From God, For Nineveh

Nineveh was one of the greatest cities of ancient times, a very large metropolitan area. Jonah describes this city as a city of three days journey.

> God said to Jonah, arise, go to Nineveh, that great city, and cry against it; for their wickedness is come up before me (Jonah 1:2).

> Because of Jonah's disobedience he found himself in the belly of a large fish for three days and three nights (Jonah 1:17).

> Jonah prayed and the Lord answered his prayer. God delivered Jonah out of the fish belly.

> God spoke unto Jonah a second time, arise, go unto Nineveh preach unto it the preaching that I bid you (Jonah 3:2).

Jonah prayed and the Lord answered his prayer. God delivered Jonah out of the fish's belly. Jonah warned the great city of Nineveh; the people believed God, and proclaimed a fast that was published through out Nineveh by the decree of the king and his nobles. No one was allowed to eat food, drink water or taste anything, this included the best herd, and flock, this fast, which was called by the king, was a serious fast.

The People Of Nineveh Repent

The people covered themselves and the animals with sackcloth and cried out unto the Lord and repented of their evil ways. Because the people repented, God also repented, in other words God relented and did not destroy Nineveh.

God is love; He doesn't get enjoyment out of killing people. But one should know that disobedience and sin will bring about destruction. God created this beautiful and perfect world, but the sin and evil doings of humans have become a permanent part of the human life.

Two Days Before Nine Eleven

I was returning my grandchildren by bus back to Rochester N.Y. where they live (I wanted them to see different cities and the scenery,) they usually fly down south to visit me. I thought a bus ride could be exciting.

My son purchased my return ticket in advance. My plan was to board the eleven o'clock bus on Monday morning September 9, 2001 but I was in for a surprise. I walked up to the bus, gave the young man my ticket, he then informed me that the bus was full. I was shocked. I stood last in line and he's now telling me to wait until the following day. I did not want to wait, so my son suggested that I stay and he would get a flight for me. I refused.

I believe God was in all of this. I was stunned; I just stood at the ticket counter. The gentleman then informed me that I had the option to instead take the New York City bus, which of course would arrive in the

New York City, three hundred miles from Rochester. In acceptance, I waited for about forty-five minutes. I boarded trailways, at the Port authority around 7:00 p.m.

I retrieved my small luggage then suddenly, I hear the voice, I knew without a doubt that it was the voice of the Lord. I heard him say "terrorist, terrorist, terrorist" three times. I began to pray a prayer in the spirit. Lord do not let the terrorist attack this place.

I do know for a surety that this makes up at the bus station was by divine intervention.

There are times when I questioned myself, beat up myself and wonder. What if I had told an officer, would he believe me? I don't know.

I feel good about making an important call to 1-800 number, being led by God. The person on the line said she understood what I was saying to her. I asked her that she believed that God speaks to people, she said yes. I asked her did she understand prophecy, she said yes. I continued my conversation with her. The following day they rounded up terrorists in South Florida, the area I had indicated. I praise God almighty.

I was very happy to have found someone who would listen to what I had to say, and not think that I was out of my mind. I felt relieved in my spirit that I chose to make that call, and give some important information to this young lady.

My prayers are always going out for the families, who lost loved ones on 9-11-2001.

A Sign From God

God established a covenant with Noah and very living thing that was with Noah. He said that He would not destroy all flesh of this earth by water again (Genesis 9:11).

But God didn't say we would not have floods.

> The token of the covenant that God made with Noah, is that He will set His bow in the cloud, and it shall be for a token of a covenant between God and Noah (Genesis 9:13).

The rainbow is a sign that we still see today.

> God did not speak to me on that Good Friday, but he did show me n open vision. My church group was returning from a shopping in Ithaca N.Y. everyone was happy and joyous, especially the young women. I was sitting on the right side of the bus, I looked out of the window, the sky was

blue no clouds in sight, suddenly I notice a long cloud, seem to be about one mile long. I yelled out to the young ladies in the back of the bus,

"Look! Look! It's a cross." Everyone got quiet, I do not know what they were thinking or feeling, but my eyes were glued to that cross that covered miles, and you know what, no one was on the cross for we know what He is risen.

A young man said to Mary Magdalene, Mary the mother of James and Salome, be not [amazed] you seek Jesus of Nazareth, who was crucified; He is risen; He is not here. Behold the place where they laid him (Mark 16:6).

God Speaks When We Least Expect

June 2002 early in the morning, I decided to pull weeds from around my flowers, though I do not have a green thumb, I do try my hand at growing plants. Many of my plants have died, but I am not giving up. I have faith that one day I will have beautiful plants growing in my yard. This was a beautiful morning, the sky was blue, I didn't notice any clouds; I heard this voice, it was the Lord, He said to me that a spirit had been released to destroy the marriages of Christians. Well, the only enemy of the Christians is Satan; if he succeeds it will be devastating. But we know that, there are some strong Christians who are rooted and groomed in the word of God, having strong faith in God, and are refusing to let Satan destroy their marriage, no matter what he sends their way.

God Instituted Marriage

Before God created a wife for Adam, he said, it is not good that the man should be alone; I will make him and help meet for him (Gen. 2:18).

Marriage is honorable, marriage is having a connection with Christ Jesus, loving Him with all of your heart, mind and soul, loving your wife or husband with the love of God, obeying God's word, praying and fasting, believing that God's word is truth, trusting in His word and not doubting when problem arises, I know for a surety that God will keep that marriage intact.

The problem with marriages today is that, the flesh is warring with the spirit and most Christian are giving in the flesh instead of obeying the spirit, their idea is whatever the flesh desires, go for it.

The Apostle Peter tells us to abstain from fleshly lusts which war against the soul (1st Peter 2:11).

Love And Respect Is A Must In The Christian Marriage

(1) Husband and wife must have a deep love for God; love themselves, and love one another and with the help of God they will be able to stand against the attack of the devil.

(2) Prayer should be an integral part of their lives.

Listed below are scriptures that are inspiring and helpful to both husband and wife.

- Whoso findeth a wife findeth a good thing, and obtaineth favor from the Lord (Proverbs 18:22).

- House and riches are the inheritance of fathers, and a prudent wife is from the Lord. (A wise woman. Proverbs 19:14).

- For the husband is the head of the wife even as Christ is the head of the church, and is the savior of the body (Ephesians 5:23).
- Husbands love your wives even as Christ also loved the church, and gave himself for it (Ephesians 5:25).
- So ought man to love their wives as their own bodies, He that loveth himself (Ephesians 5:28).
- In like manner, ye husbands dwell with your wife according to knowledge, giving honor unto the weaker vessel, and of being heirs together of the grace of life, that your prayers be not hindered (1st Peter 3:7)
- A virtuous woman is a crown to her husband, but she that maketh ashamed is as rottenness in his bones.
- Husbands and wives must submit yourselves one to another in the fear of God (Ephesians 5:21).
- Wives, submit yourselves unto your own husbands, as unto the Lord (Ephesians 5:22).
- Therefore as the church is subject unto Christ, so let the wives be unto their own husbands in everything (Ephesians 5:24).
- Likewise you wives be in subjection to your

own husbands: that if any obey not the word, they also may without the word be won by the conversation of the wives.

Respect And Obedience Is Not One Sided

Husbands know that your wives are not slaves, but are your help-meet. Wives understand this one thing, your husband is the head of the wife, he is not your son; we cannot change anyone, only God has the power to change the way we act or think. We must have respect for one another, obey the teachings of Christ and reap the benefit of a marriage that is pleasing to God.

When the marriage is solid, the children will grow up having respect for their companions. In most marriages, children tend to emulate their parents. Parents must strive to be good examples for their offspring.

Today, we have fathers "hangin' out"; mother's partying, everybody doing their own thing. In most cases, children are raising themselves.

There are no moral values in some of the homes today.

Satan Is Fishing For Our Children

God created male and female and He blessed them and said unto them, be fruitful and multiply (Genesis 1:28), in other words, God was saying to man, produce children.

Satan had a plan from the beginning to destroy the children, he is just lurking, and waiting around for the right time to implement his plan, he is fishing for large number of our youth and he is pulling in the net.

Many of our children, grandchildren and or relative children have gotten caught in Satan's net. Only a few people are trying to do something to save your people. We have sat around much too long, not doing anything, not saying anything; now that things have gotten out of control we are just stunned.

I can see why God is displeased; this world is in a mess.

Know What Your Children Are Doing

Are your children watching movies, videos, games that glorify murder, Satanic, demonic witches, profanity, explicit sexual acts and the demoralization of women? If you answer yes to one of the above, you need to pray and talk to your child, take control of the situation immediately, do whatever is necessary, go to your Pastor if you feel your child needs some form of counseling.

> Godly instruction is given to us in scripture. Train up a child in the way he should go and, when he is old, he will not depart from it (Proverbs 22:6).

Finally, children must be taught to love and respect self as well as others.

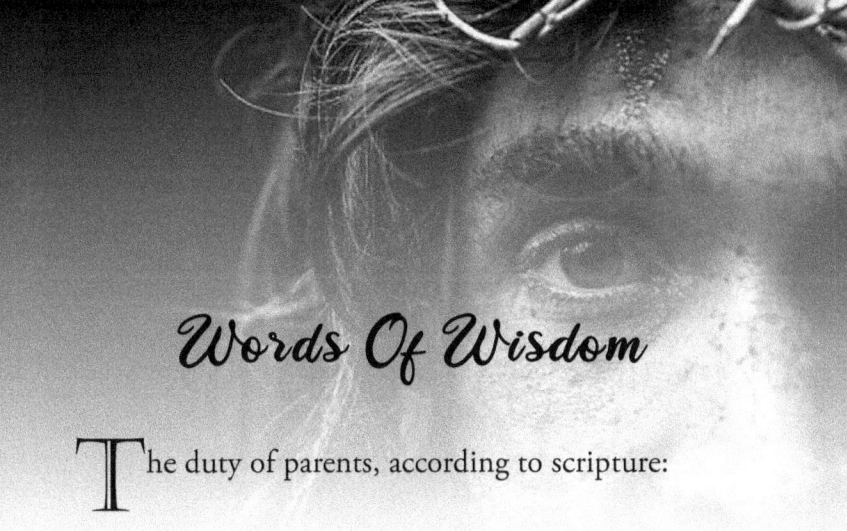

Words Of Wisdom

The duty of parents, according to scripture:

- He that spareth his rod hateth his son; but he that loveth him chasteneth him [early] (Proverbs 13:24).
- Chasten thy son while there is hope, and let not thy soul spare for crying (Proverbs 19:18).
- Train up a child in the way he should go and, when he is old, he will not depart from it (Proverbs 22:6).
- Foolishness is bound in the heart of a child, but the rod of correction shall drive it far from him (Proverbs 22:15).
- Withhold not correction from the child; for it thou beatest him with the rod, he shall not die (Proverbs 23:13).

- The rod and reproof give wisdom, but a child left to himself bringeth his mother to shame (Proverbs 29:15).
- Correct thy son, and he shall give thee rest; yea, he shall give delight unto thy soul (Proverbs 29:17).
- And you fathers provoke not your children to wrath, but bring them up in the nature and abomination of the Lord (Ephesians 6:4).

But if any provide not for his own, and specially for those of his own house, he hath denied the faith, and is worst than an infidel (1 Timothy 5:8).

Children Must Be Obedient To Parent

This is a commandment of God. So many of our young people today are so disrespectful, they do not listen to their parents, they use profanity (cussing or foul language), they smoke drink, gamble and are doing everything that is contrary to the word of God. On the other hand, we do have children today, who are good; saved children doing everything to live a Christian life.

The Apostle Paul gives us instructions for the believers:

(1) Children, obey your parents in the Lord; for this is right.

(2) Honor your father and mother (which is the first commandment with promise) that it may be well with thee and thou may live long on the earth.

Who Is Responsible For The Spiritual Decline In America

> Be sober, be vigilant, because your adversary, the devil, like a roaring lion walketh about, seeking whom he may devour (1st Peter 5:8).

Not only in America, but all over the world, Satan and his helpers are trying to destroy the human race. We know that this time is already prepared for him and his cohorts.

(Revelation 20:10 states), And the Devil that deceived them was cast into the lake of fire and brimstone, where the beast and the false prophet are, and shall be tormented day and night forever and ever.

The instigator Satan will be tormented for all eternity.

We must confess, to playing a part in all that is happening around us today.

(1) The parent is guilty because they didn't do their job.
(2) The body of Christ is guilty because they didn't do their job.
(3) The Government is guilty because they didn't do their job.

There is enough blame to go around. Now that everything is out of control, everyone is passing the buck. Though we do have some good people in the body of Christ working to save our young people; and there are some good people in government.

But are we doing enough? As I have said earlier, things have gotten out of hand. May God have mercy on all of us.

There is Life After Death

There's life after death, according to scripture Jesus was resurrected, and there are many infallible proof.

❖ 1st Corinthians 15:20-23

On the first day of his resurrection, Jesus appeared to Mary Magdalene, a woman whom he had cast out of seven Demons.

❖ Mark 16:9-11, John 20:11-18

Meanwhile, Mary the mother of James, Salome, and the other woman entered the tomb and saw an angel who assured them that Jesus had risen.

❖ Mark 28:8-10

Jesus had appeared to Peter.

❖ Luke 24:34, 1st Corinthians 15:5

He had appeared in another form unto two who had been walking with him.

❖ Mark 16:12

These two men are called the Emmaus disciples; they did not recognize Jesus until he revealed himself to them.

❖ Mark 16:12; Luke 24;13-32

Jesus appeared unto the eleven as they sat eating, and upbraided them with their unbelief and hardness of heart, because they believed not those who had seen him after he had risen.

❖ Mark 16:14; Luke 24:36-43; John 20:19-25

After eight days, Jesus appeared again to the disciples, this time doubting Thomas was present.

The amazing thing about Jesus' visit to the disciples was that he walked through the walls. Jesus standing in the midst of them allowed Thomas to touch, and place his hand into his side.

Jesus had all power and that he was able to change his appearance and walk through walls. After this life we will be able to do the same.

Why am I saying this? Well the answer I have, cam from God Himself.

A Dream From God

And it shall come to pass in the last days, saith God, I will pour out my spirit upon all flesh; and your sons and daughters shall prophesy, and your old men shall dream dreams (Act 2:17).

In a dream in 1999, I had an amazing experience. I saw a celestial being that happened to be me. I was looking at this being from another area, it seemed like I was having an out of body experience. I was actually looking at myself in my spiritual body.

As I began to speak from this celestial body. I said, will I be able to feel? Actually, I was talking to the Lord. This was all happening in a beautiful garden. As I willed myself to move downward, out of midair, my feet touched the ground, which was covered with beautiful stone.

I know for a surety, that we will have the power to will oneself form one location to another.

The word of God stated, there is celestial bodies and terrestrial bodies, but the glory of the celestial is one, and the glory of the terrestrial is another. The saints of God will have a celestial body. 1st Corinthians 15:40 states that flesh and blood cannot enter the kingdom of God.

The apostle Paul made it very clear to the church of Corinth in 1st Corinthians 12:51; 52;53; Behold, I show you a mystery; we shall not all sleep, but we shall all be changed;

For this corruption must put incorruption, and this mortal must put on immortality. This body will be raised in power; it will suffer no more death, pain and suffering, oh what a glorious day that he will be.

The apostle Paul states in verse 52, that we shall be changed in a moment, in the twinkling of an eye. In other words, this change will be instantaneous. Oh what a powerful God we serve. Only a fool would refuse to serve the true and living God, who has promised eternal life to the believers. I believe totally in the word of God, nothing less.

Luke 23:42-43 states that the repentant thief on the cross was saved when he said unto Jesus, Lord remember me when thou come into your kingdom.

And Jesus said unto the thief, today shall you be with me in paradise.

On that day, the male factor died a physical death on the cross but his soul and spirit were with the Lord.

We, as Christians, should rejoice knowing that after death we will be present with the Lord.

Heaven Is Real

The life we live will determine where we spend eternity, the choice is ours. The word of God given instruction on how to live this Christian life.

My choice it to live a life that is pleasing to God, so that I will meet Him face to face one day.

I must say that Heaven is real, according to the words of Christ.

> Whosoever, therefore, shall break one of these least commandments, and shall teach men so, he shall be called the least in the kingdom of heaven, but whosoever shall teach them, they shall be called great in the kingdom of Heaven (Mark 5:19).

> For I say unto you that except your righteousness shall exceed the righteousness of the scribed and Pharisees, you shall in no case enter the kingdom of heaven.

> Jesus says to his disciples, that you may be the sons of your father, who is in heaven; for the sun to rise on the evil and on the unjust (Mark 5:45).

Jesus instruction in prayer included the word heaven, he told the disciples to pray after this manner:

> Our father who art in heaven, hallowed be thy name (Mark 6:9).
>
> Our heavenly father's dwelling place is in heaven... 1st Kings 8:30; Psalms 115:3; 123:1; Ezekiel 1:1; Mark 6:10; Acts 7:49; Hebrew 8:1: Revelations 4:1.
>
> Heaven is called the third heaven, the abode of God, it is called paradise; which was promised by Christ to the penitent thief... Luke 23:43. Apostle Paul was caught up into the third heaven (2nd Corinthians 12:4).
>
> We have the ascension of Christ... Luke 24:50; John 14:2; Acts 1:9; 2:33; Romans 8:34; 1st Peter 3:22.

There will be joy and much happiness in heaven, Psalms 16:11 states, thou will show me the path of life. In the presence in fullness of joy; at the right hand, there are pleasures for evermore.

> Corinthians 2:9; 1st Peter 1:4; Revelation 7:16; 14:13; 21:4; 22:3.
>
> God has said in his word, but as it is written, eye has not seen, nor ears heard, neither have entered into the heart of man, the things which God has prepared for them that love me (1st Corinthians 2:9).

In 1989 as I sat in the Choir. I noticed a bright beam, (a light) it was as if heaven had opened up. I looked upward there was no ending, the beam was in front of me, and directly behind a young lady, I said to her, do you have a back problem, she said yes, I said God healed you. Prior to seeing this vision, we were praising God; just imagine being in heaven praising God, oh what a time that would be. Supernatural things are revealed to many Christians. I am just one of many who loves the Lord.

> Verse 10. But God has revealed them unto us by his spirit; for the spirit searcheth all things, yea the deep things of God.

> Verse 11. For what man knoweth the things of a man [except] the spirit of a man which is in him? Even so the things of God knoweth no man, but the spirit of God.

> Verse 12. Now we have received, not the spirit of the world, but the spirit who is of God; that we might know the things that are freely given to us of God.

> From the beginning of creation, God has spoken to man, for man was made in his image (Genesis 1:26).

There Is A Place Called Hell

In the teachings of Jesus, we know for a fact that hell is going to be a place for eternal punishment for those who sin and are wicked. Jesus promised that he will pronounce sentence.

> In the book of the prophet Isaiah he states, for their worm does not die and their fire is not quenched (Isaiah 66:24).

Jesus solemn warning of hell, and if thy hand offend thee, cut it off, it is better for thee to enter into life maimed than, having two hands, to go into hell, into the fire that never shall be quenched...Mark 9:43; 44; 45; 46; 47; 48.

Hell is not a place where you would find a devil that is dressed in red, with horns and a pitchfork. Know that it is a place of much suffering.

I do personally believe that there is a place called hell. In 1989, I had a near death experience, I was a patient in Myers memorial hospital in Buffalo N.Y, giving birth to my third son. The labor was long and intense. At some point. I stopped breathing, the oxygen didn't work in my room, I remember falling through a dark tunnel. I heard the Doctor and nurse calling my name and slapping me on my face, but I was not able to respond. I was told the following morning a doctor ran two or three flights of stairs, and hand carried one of those large green oxygen tanks, I believe God used this man to save my life. The nurse said that they almost lost me. Personally, I believe without a doubt, that I was on my way to hell. I was not serving God, hadn't been to Church in years, didn't think about him, actually I had backslid. Oh but I thank him for giving me another chance.

God is a God of love, He will do the same for you, He will open His arms and receive you unto the family of God.

The apostle Peter states in 2nd Peter 2:4. For if God spare not the angels that sinned, but cast them down to hell, and delivered them into chains of judgement. Also Jude 6, and the angels which kept not their first estate, but their own habitation, he had reserved in everlasting chains under darkness unto the judgement of that great day.

Jesus described hell as a literal place in the heart of this earth.

For as Jonas was three days and three nights in the belly of the fish. (Jonas 1:17).

The purpose of hell is to retain the souls of the wicked until Judgement Day.

The apostle John states in revelation 20:14,

> And I saw a great white throne, and him that sat on it, from whose face the earth the heaven fled away; and there was found no place for them. And I saw the dead, small and great, stand before God; and the books were opened, and the dead were judged out of those things, which were written in the books according to their works. And the sea gave up the dead, which was in it; and death and hell delivered up the dead, which were in them; and they were judged every man according to their works.

> And death and hell were cast into the lake of fire. This is the second death (Revelation 20:14). The final hell is called "Gehenna" (Greek) or the Lake of Fire (English). And whosoever was not found written in the book of life was cast into the lake of fire (Revelations 20:15).

The Ultimate Destination

The final destination of Satan and the wicked will be in the lake of fire. Satan is doing everything within his limited power to destroy and to cause havoc on God's earth. We know that his time is running out.

> We know according to scripture that lake of fire was prepared for the devil and his angels…Mark 25:41.

> Then shall he say, also to unto them on the left hand, depart from me, ye cursed, into everlasting fire, prepared for the devil and his angels (Mark 25:41).

A Vision Of The Lake Of Fire

God revealed to me in an open vision in 1982, as I was reading the word of God, when suddenly I saw a lake of fire, the fire seem to be moving like water, liquid fire. There was no flame, just fire. I closed and opened my eyes thinking maybe this is not real; I turned my head in different directions after the third time the vision disappeared.

There is no doubt in my mind that there is a lake of fire. God revealed this to me years before I read it in his words.

As a believer, I believe with every ounce of my being, that God's word is truth, and we know that God's word stands on its own.

Salvation Is A Gift From God

I pray for the unsaved souls, I know that God is still waiting for you to accept him as your personal savior, he saved me from eternal damnation, and he will do the same for you.

You do not need to pay for salvation, Christ paid it all on Cavalry. You have been given a free gift; no credit card or cash is needed.

All you have to do is accept Christ as your personal savior.

> Listen to what Jesus says to Nicodemus a Pharisees, "Verily, verily I say unto you, except a man be born again, he cannot see the kingdom of God" (John 3:3).
>
> Verse 5. Verily, verily I say unto you, except a man be born of water and of spirit, he cannot enter into the kingdom of God.
>
> Verse 6. That which is born of flesh is flesh, and that which is born of spirit is spirit.

Verse 17. For God sent not his son into the world to condemn the world, but that he world through him (Christ) might be saved.

My prayer is that every unsaved reader of this book gives his or her life to Christ.